Happy Flowers

COLORING BOOK

Color Yourself Happy!

Original Illustrations
by Debbie Vinyard

this BOOK BeLONGs to

• • • • • • • • • • • • • •

Printed by CreateSpace, an Amazon.com company

ISBN: 978-1539709138

Created by Debbie Vinyard
Happy 1st, LLC
www.happyfirst.com

Welcome!

I hope you enjoy coloring my flowers as much as I've enjoyed creating them for you. The simple truth is that drawing makes me happy, and I want to to spread the happiness. Coloring calms the mind and helps with stress, grief, sadness, or anything else that might be dragging us down. It also allows us to briefly escape from the digital world, which we all need to do once in a while. I live on 40 acres in Oklahoma with my husband, a partially blind cat and two three-legged dogs, but even I feel the need to disconnect now and again.

These are my original designs, all of which I drew by hand. I've included a range of designs, some simple, some more complex. I put one design per page (blank on the back) so you can cut out and frame your creations. You can see how I color on my Facebook page (I tend to go outside of the lines), but use YOUR imagination and be YOU! I believe everyone is creative, so be yourself and see where it takes you.

I would love to see your art and share it with others! You can connect with me at debbie@happyfirst.com, facebook.com/debbievinyardartist, twitter.com/debbievinyard, and instagram.com/debbievinyard. You can also join my email list at www.happyfirst.com to be the first to know of new designs and/or coloring books, plus other fun stuff such as free exclusive downloads.

If you share your creations on social media, please use the hashtag #myhappyflowers so we can all enjoy them.

Color yourself happy!

 Deb

P.S. If you enjoy this coloring book, I would really appreciate a rating and review on Amazon to help others find it too!

✿ ✿ ✿ special thanks ✿ ✿ ✿

Some of my designs I just make up and some I draw based on flower arrangements I have seen.

I would like to thank the following florists for their inspiration and support.

Dr Delphinium Designs (Dallas, Texas)
Farmgirl Flowers (San Francisco, CA)
Stems Florist (Tulsa, OK)
Toni's Flowers & Gifts (Tulsa, OK)

Thanks so much, you all are very talented!

And most of all I want to thank my husband, Randy, for his constant encouragement, and for seeing in me what I couldn't see in myself.

test ❀ Page

Test your pens, pencils and markers on this page.

Some tips:

❀ If you are worried about ink bleeding through the page, place a piece of cardboard or thick paper behind the page you are coloring to soak up up the extra ink.

❀ If using pencils, the tip above will also help stop pressure marks.

❀ Some of my simpler designs lend well to brush markers, my favorite being Copic markers. Watercolor pencils may work well too.

Happy Coloring!

♡ Deb

1

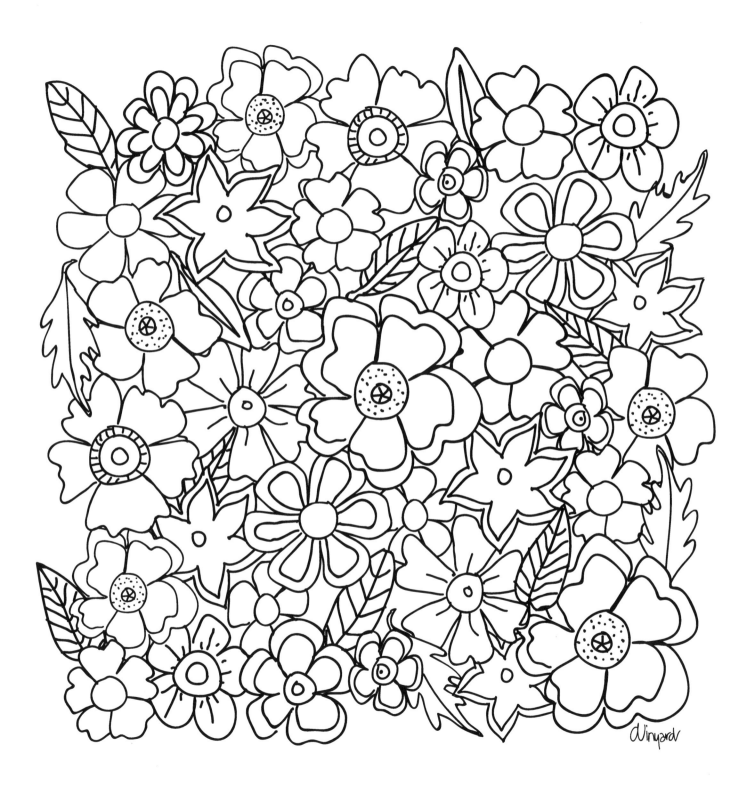

1

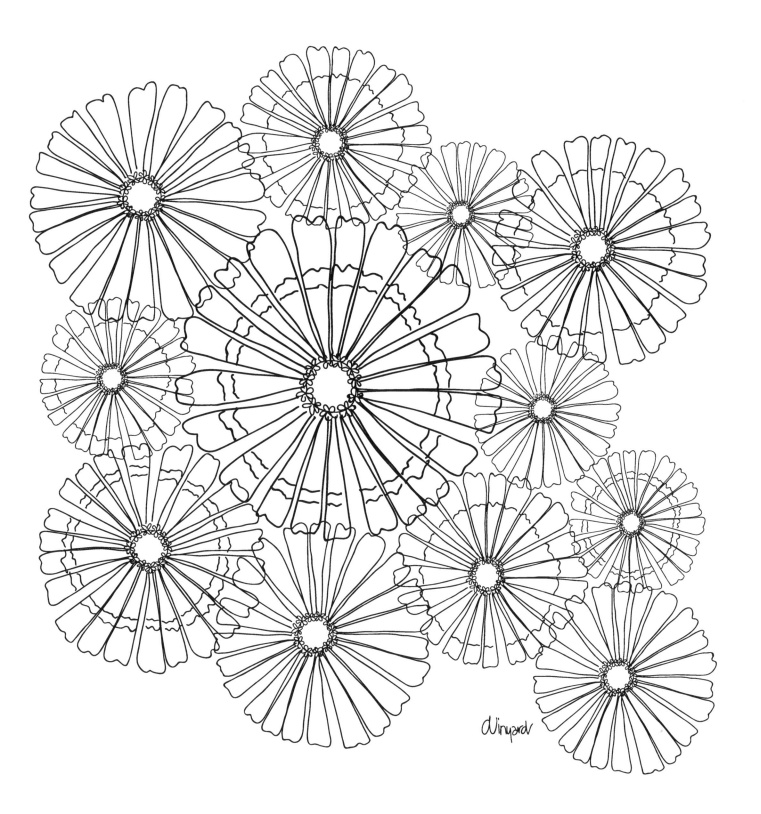

Made in the USA
Columbia, SC
14 October 2024

43642299R00037